CEOs & Suicide

The Invisible Game of Leadership

Joshua Christopherson

Contents

Introduction..**9**

Chapter 1: The Invisible Game **13**

The two games every leader plays

Chapter 2: The Loneliest Seat **21**

Isolation and emotional containment

Chapter 3: Headwinds..**29**

Pressure as a condition of growth

Chapter 4: IMC (Flying in the Clouds) **37**

Leading without visibility

Chapter 5: Payroll Before My Own Bills **43**

The moral weight of responsibility

Chapter 6: Managing Personalities.............................**49**

Emotional labor and regulation

Chapter 7: Selling Rainbows and Unicorns **55**

Why mindset precedes strategy

Chapter 8: Purple Cows..**63**

Humanity, creativity, and culture

Chapter 9: The Buyback Spiral....................................**69**

Compounding crises and distortion

Chapter 10: The Waterfall..**75**

The logic trap of removal

Chapter 11: The Call That Saved Me **83**

Interruption and connection

Chapter 12: Values in a Crisis **89**

Integrity under pressure

Chapter 13: Turning Skyward **95**

Sustainable leadership after survival

Epilogue **105**

About the Author **107**

Acknowledgements **109**

Leadership Checklist **111**

Introduction

Crabbing Into the Wind

The flight from Spanish Fork to Nephi is short. On a calm day, it barely feels like a flight at all. Just enough time to climb, level off, and start thinking about the approach.

I had flown this route before. Familiar airspace. Familiar terrain. My sister was with me, heading home to my parents' house. It should have been routine.

That's the thing about flying, and leadership.

Most of the hardest moments don't announce themselves in advance.

As we got closer to Nephi, the winds started picking up. Not unusual for that area, but stronger than forecast. Snow began falling, not drifting down, but moving sideways, almost horizontal. Visibility was still acceptable, but tightening. The kind of conditions that demand attention without yet demanding panic.

Runway 17 was active.

On approach, the crosswind made itself known immediately. Strong enough that lining up with the runway meant not pointing at it at all. I had to crab into the wind, nose pointed off to the side, while tracking straight toward the numbers.

If you've never experienced it, it's disorienting.

The runway isn't in front of you.

It's out the side window, almost over the right wing.

Your instincts scream that something is wrong.

Everything in you wants to fix the picture, to straighten out, to make it look normal. But normal is the wrong move. Normal will drift you off the runway. Normal will lose the fight.

So you trust your training.

You keep flying the airplane.

You accept the picture that feels wrong.

You stay calm while the ground comes closer.

This is where panic makes things worse. Overcorrecting. Freezing. Letting fear drive inputs instead of data. You don't get loud in moments like this. You get focused.

I remember how quiet the cockpit felt, the kind of quiet where every control input matters. Where you're not thinking about anything else. Not work. Not problems. Not tomorrow. Just airspeed, alignment, timing.

There's a moment, right before touchdown, where everything has to come together. You kick out the crab. Align the aircraft. Set it down firmly and cleanly. Not gracefully… decisively.

And then, suddenly, you're on the ground.

Taxiing. Breathing again.

From the outside, it probably looked like a normal landing. No one on the ramp would have known how much work it took to arrive there safely. No applause. No acknowledgment.

Just another airplane that landed.

That's leadership.

Most people only see the landing.

They don't see the wind.

They don't see the corrections.

They don't see the strain of holding steady when everything feels slightly off.

They don't see the part where you're looking out the side window, trusting that what feels wrong is actually what's keeping you on course.

This book is about that part.

It's about flying when conditions aren't ideal.

About staying composed when the picture doesn't look right.

About leading when the pressure is real and the margin is thin.

And about the truth every pilot learns early, but every leader has to rediscover for themselves:

You don't take off, or land, by running with the wind.

You turn into it.

Chapter 1

The Invisible Game

Every CEO plays two games.

The first is visible.

Revenue. Growth. Headcount. Market share. Culture decks. Board meetings. The metrics investors track and LinkedIn celebrates. This is the game everyone sees, judges, and comments on.

The second game is invisible.

It happens before your feet hit the floor in the morning.

It shows up in the silence after a hard conversation.

It lives in the space between midnight and 3:00 a.m., when you're staring at the ceiling running numbers that don't quite work and replaying decisions you can't undo.

The invisible game is where leadership actually lives.

And almost no one talks about it.

From the outside, leadership looks like confidence. From the inside, it often feels like pressure, constant, quiet, unrelenting pressure. The kind that doesn't go away when the office lights turn off. The kind you carry home, even when you promise yourself you won't.

If you're a founder or CEO reading this, especially in the $5-$50M range, you know exactly what I mean. You've grown past the scrappy startup phase, but you're not big enough to disappear behind layers of executives. Decisions still land squarely on your shoulders.

Payroll still has your name on it. Culture still rises or falls with your mood, your words, your energy.

You're visible.

But the pressure you carry is not.

Here's the part no one prepares you for: as the company grows, your margin for honesty shrinks.

You can't say out loud that cash flow scares you this week, or that you might not be able to take a paycheck. (Yes, I've run a $10M-a-year business and skipped my own pay to make sure employees, some making more than me, got paid.)

You can't admit you're not sure the strategy will work.

You can't show how tired you are, because people are watching you to decide whether they should be worried.

So you do what leaders do.

You put it on.

You show up.

You project certainty.

And slowly, almost imperceptibly, the invisible game starts to cost you more than the visible one ever could.

The Cost of Looking Put Together

I never planned to be a CEO. I didn't chase the title. I didn't grow up dreaming about running a company.

I grew up around airplanes. My world was aviation. My dad was a flight instructor and corporate pilot. My grandfather worked for the FAA. My uncle flew for FedEx. Flying was the plan.

Sales was just supposed to be a way to pay for college, but somewhere along the way I was hooked by the paychecks and success.

It wasn't long before a manager suggested I fully commit and use my success to buy my own small plane. Essentially allowing me to fly for fun but still earn a high income and avoid the life of a professional pilot, always away from home and family.

That idea got me excited and I committed to a new life direction.

Twelve years later, I was still in sales, but as a manager and leader. Sometimes doing great. Other times wondering how the bills were going to get paid. I worked under a lot of CEOs during those years, paying attention to what I respected, what I didn't, which decisions felt right, and which ones felt disconnected from reality.

I never imagined I'd get my own turn.

When I was eventually asked to step into the CEO role at Achieve Today, I didn't want it. We had already hired two CEOs over the years. I had sat in one-on-one meetings with a previous CEO who told me he was about to go out and tell employees not to come back the next day because we wouldn't make payroll.

I convinced him we could survive the week. I made a plan. We made it.

Years later my partner, Aaron, believed I was the right person for the job. He felt it was time to stop looking for experts outside the company and have faith in ourselves.

I wasn't so sure.

I knew how heavy the seat was.

I knew what it cost.

What I didn't understand yet was how quiet that cost would be.

As CEO, you become the emotional shock absorber for the entire organization. Stress flows downhill until it hits you, and then it has nowhere else to go. You absorb fear, frustration, disappointment, anger, and uncertainty. You translate chaos into calm, even when you don't feel calm yourself.

There's an unspoken rule in leadership:

Your emotions are contagious, so you better control them.

I've come to believe this is true. Psychology is contagious. Energy spreads faster than strategy. But the unintended consequence is that many leaders learn to suppress instead of process. We learn to perform stability rather than build it internally.

That's where the invisible game starts to turn dangerous.

The Calmest Person in the Room

One of the most important leadership lessons I've learned didn't come from business school or a boardroom. It came from aviation.

Every pilot learns this early:

If you run with the wind, you can't take off.

You have to turn into it. Face it.

The very thing you push against is what lifts you up.

Flying teaches something leadership eventually demands: calm is not the absence of fear, it's the management of it.

I learned this the hard way.

As a teenager, I was flying with my dad when we blew a cylinder mid-flight in a snowstorm. Whiteout conditions. Engine failure. Real consequences.

I still remember how calm he was. Methodical. Focused. Training over emotion. One checklist at a time.

I remember looking out the right window from the front seat and watching the prop feather and come to a stop, something you never expect to see in flight.

Years later, in my own high-performance aircraft, I had a gear failure on approach. Electric gear stuck. Manual pump required. High workload. No room for panic. I had to fly the plane, manage the emergency, and land safely.

Leadership feels the same, almost daily.

Not the absence of stress, but the ability to stay composed inside it.

One quote has guided how I lead ever since:

IN THE CHAOS, LOOK FOR THE CALMEST PERSON IN THE ROOM.

THAT'S YOUR LEADER.

The mistake many CEOs make is assuming calm means you don't feel the chaos. The truth is calm comes from knowing how to hold it without letting it leak everywhere.

You're Not Doing It Wrong

Years ago, I met regularly with Greg, a seasoned CEO who had built and scaled a massive solar company, thousands of employees, hundreds of millions in funding. One week, after reviewing our P&Ls, I admitted I couldn't understand why we couldn't seem to turn the corner.

I expected advice. Maybe criticism.

Instead, he smiled and said:

"Josh, you aren't doing anything wrong. The same hard choices and challenges you're struggling with are the same ones I struggle with as CEO. You just add a few more zeros to your numbers."

That sentence changed me.

Because one of the most dangerous lies in the invisible game is this:

If I were better, this wouldn't be this hard.

Leadership at scale is hard. Period. The stress you feel is not proof of inadequacy, it's evidence of responsibility. But when you're alone with it, it's easy to confuse weight with weakness.

This book exists to break that confusion.

What This Book Is Really About

This is not a book about building a company.

It's a book about surviving leadership.

It's about imposter syndrome, inadequacy, fear, and the quiet moments where you question whether you're the right person for the job. It's about the pressure to look strong when you feel anything but. It's about the nights no one sees and the decisions no one applauds.

And yes, it's about suicide. Not as shock value, but as a reality too many leaders flirt with silently when the invisible game overwhelms them.

Every chapter ahead offers something practical, frameworks, checklists, perspectives you can actually use. But more importantly, it gives language to experiences you've probably never said out loud.

Because the goal isn't to make leadership easy.

The goal is to make it sustainable.

And like flying, sustainability starts by turning into the wind.

Chapter 2

The Loneliest Seat

No one warns you how lonely leadership becomes.

Not "I don't have friends" lonely.

Not "I wish I had more time" lonely.

A different kind of lonely.

The kind where you're surrounded by people all day and still feel completely alone with the things that matter most.

When you become a CEO, something subtle changes in your relationships. Conversations begin to filter themselves. People watch your reactions more closely. Words get chosen more carefully around you. Even well-intentioned honesty starts to soften at the edges.

You notice it, but you don't call it out.

Because calling it out would make it worse.

So you adapt.

You stop sharing uncertainty.

You stop venting.

You stop thinking out loud.

Not because you want to be distant, but because you're protecting the system. You understand that your emotional state doesn't just belong to you anymore. It ripples.

Psychology is contagious. Faster than the flu.

And once you understand that, you start to self-contain.

The Shrinking Circle

As a CEO, your circle of safe honesty gets very small, very fast.

You can't talk openly with employees. They need confidence, not your fears.

You can't fully unload on your leadership team. They already carry enough weight, and you don't want to destabilize them.

You can't always talk to friends outside the business. They don't understand the stakes, or worse, they oversimplify them.

"Just shut it down."

"Just raise prices."

"Just fire people."

Easy advice when payroll isn't on your shoulders and you don't care about the people you employ.

Over time, you start carrying more internally. You tell yourself it's just part of the job. That strength means silence. That leaders don't complain. That this is what responsibility feels like.

And in a way, that's true.

But silence without release doesn't create strength.

It creates pressure.

And pressure, without an outlet, eventually looks for one.

The Performance of Certainty

There's another unspoken rule of leadership:

You don't get to have two bad days in a row.

I used to say this to myself constantly. Not as motivation, but as survival.

Leaders don't have two good days in a row either. The hill is always higher. The resistance is always stronger. The problems don't politely wait until you're rested.

I didn't become a leader because it was easy.

I became a leader because I believed it was right.

But believing it's right doesn't make it light.

So you learn to perform certainty.

You walk into meetings with answers you're still forming.

You reassure teams while running scenarios in your head.

You give motivational talks while quietly wondering if you're missing something obvious.

From the outside, it looks like confidence.

From the inside, it feels like acting.

And the longer you do it without relief, the harder it becomes to tell where the performance ends, and you begin.

The Person Who Never Left

Through all of this, there was one person who never stopped seeing me.

Not the CEO.

Not the leader.

Not the guy with answers.

My wife, Raelene.

She has been my rock through every version of this journey. She didn't just support the business, she supported the human carrying it.

She brought reality when I drifted into worst-case thinking.

She brought calm when I was overwhelmed. She brought love when I felt like I was failing.

She also sacrificed more than anyone will ever see.

Missed bills.

Late nights.

Unspoken stress.

Moments when the weight followed me home and sat at our dinner table.

Times when I wasn't fully present, even when I was physically there.

She stayed strong when I didn't feel strong.

She believed when I doubted.

She loved me when I didn't like myself very much.

This book is dedicated to her.

Every leader needs at least one person who doesn't benefit from your confidence, but loves you anyway.

Find that person.

Strength Isn't Silence

One of the biggest leadership myths is that strength means carrying everything alone.

Real strength is knowing where you can safely put the weight down.

For me, that was my wife.

And eventually, my business partner, Aaron.

Aaron has always been a steady presence, optimistic, grounded, resilient. He believed in me long before I believed in myself. And yet, even with him, I didn't share everything. Not at first. Not when things were darkest.

Not because he couldn't handle it.

Because I didn't think I could afford to be seen struggling.

That's the trap.

You start protecting other people from your truth, and slowly, you lose access to it yourself.

The Two-Person Rule

In aviation, there's a principle used in high-risk environments called the two-person rule. Certain actions can't be taken alone. Not because you're incompetent, but because humans under pressure can make catastrophic decisions in isolation.

Leadership needs the same rule.

Every CEO needs at least one person who has permission to ask the real question:

"How are you actually doing?"

Not "How's the business?"

Not "What's the plan?"

But you.

And that person needs the authority to not accept "I'm fine" as an answer.

Because "I'm fine" is often the most dangerous sentence a leader says.

The Invisible Cost

The invisible game doesn't usually break leaders publicly.

It breaks them quietly.

It shows up as irritability.

As exhaustion.

As numbness.

As the feeling that no matter how much you achieve, it's never enough.

Work becomes love made visible, but also obligation made relentless.

And if you don't name it, don't share it, don't manage it, it doesn't go away.

It compounds.

Just like stress in an aircraft, ignored warnings don't mean safety.

They mean delayed consequences.

What This Chapter Is Really Saying

If you take nothing else from this chapter, take this:

You are not weak for feeling alone in leadership.

You are not broken because this is hard.

And you are not meant to play the invisible game by yourself.

Strength isn't silence.

Strength is structure.

Who knows the real you?

Who can interrupt your worst thinking?

Who has permission to tell you the truth when you're spiraling?

If you don't know the answers yet, that's okay.

We'll build them.

Chapter 3

Headwinds

Early in my flying journey, when I was about twenty-three, I took some friends flying one evening after work.

At that point, I always kept my plane fully fueled. I usually flew alone, and full tanks felt like a margin of safety. What I didn't fully account for that night was weight and balance. Four grown men in every seat changes the math, especially with full fuel.

There was a light breeze as we lined up for takeoff. Nothing concerning. We took off into the wind, exactly as I was trained to do. It was a beautiful night for flying.

But the airplane felt wrong.

It took much longer than usual to get to speed. When I finally had enough airspeed to lift off, the climb rate was sluggish, uncomfortably sluggish.

In the moment, I couldn't fully understand why.

Instinct told me to pull back harder on the yoke and force the climb. But training stopped me. I didn't have the airspeed. Pulling back would only stall the aircraft.

Then another instinct crept in, one that felt logical but wasn't.

Turn. Get the wind behind you. Let it help you.

As I started the turn, I immediately knew it was the wrong choice. Lift became harder to achieve, not easier.

Why?

Because the first thing every pilot learns is this:

If you run with the wind, you can't take off.

Your instincts tell you to go the easy direction, the direction that feels supportive. But airplanes don't work that way. To generate lift, you have to turn into the resistance. You face the wind head-on.

The very thing pushing against you is what allows you to leave the ground.

Leadership is no different.

Most CEOs don't fail because of a lack of opportunity. They fail because they misunderstand pressure. They see resistance as a sign they're doing something wrong instead of a sign they're doing something real.

Headwinds are not a defect.

They are a condition of flight.

When It Starts to Feel Heavy

There's a phase every growing company hits where the pressure suddenly feels different.

In the early days, everything is hard, but it's exciting. You're scrappy. You expect chaos. Wins feel electric. Losses sting, but you recover quickly because momentum is still building.

But somewhere between $5M and $50M, the weight changes.

You have employees with families.

You have fixed costs that don't care how motivated you are.

You have partners, vendors, leases, debt, and expectations layered on top of ambition.

The stakes are higher, but the margin for error feels smaller.

This is where many leaders start internalizing pressure instead of working with it. They begin treating stress like a personal failure instead of a leadership signal.

That's when the invisible game starts tightening.

Pressure Is Data

One of the most important shifts I had to make as a CEO was learning to reinterpret pressure.

Pressure is not punishment.

Pressure is information.

It tells you:

- Where the system is strained
- Where decisions are overdue
- Where clarity is missing
- Where alignment has drifted

But when pressure becomes constant, it's easy to stop listening to it and start fighting it emotionally.

You begin asking the wrong questions:

Why is this happening to me?

Why can't I catch a break?

Why does it feel like I'm always behind?

Those questions don't create lift.

They create fatigue.

A better question, the one pilots ask, is this:

What is this condition requiring of me right now?

Different winds demand different responses.

Crabbing vs. Fighting

In aviation, you don't fight a crosswind by overpowering it. You don't muscle the airplane into submission.

You work with the physics.

You crab into the wind.

You accept that the picture looks wrong.

You stay aligned with where you're actually going, not where you wish you were pointed.

This is where many leaders struggle.

They want things to look right:

- Culture should feel positive all the time
- Numbers should move in clean, predictable lines
- Teams should stay motivated without constant recalibration

But real leadership often looks messy from the inside.

Sometimes alignment requires uncomfortable conversations.

Sometimes progress creates temporary morale dips.

Sometimes stability means making decisions that won't be understood immediately.

If you try to make leadership look right instead of be right, you'll drift.

Calm Is a Discipline

People often assume calm leaders don't feel stress.

That's wrong.

Calm leaders feel stress deeply, they just don't let it hijack their behavior.

I've learned that calm isn't a personality trait. It's a practiced discipline. One you earn through repetition, perspective, and hard experience.

There were times, especially during our hardest seasons, when cash flow was tight, revenue unpredictable, and decisions carried real consequences. Weeks where one misstep could ripple through the entire company.

In those moments, I kept coming back to a principle I now live by:

In the chaos, look for the calmest person in the room.

That's your leader.

Not the loudest.

Not the most emotional.

Not the most reactive.

The calmest.

That doesn't mean detached. It means grounded. Regulated enough to think clearly when others can't.

Emotional Regulation Is a Leadership Skill

No one tells you this when you step into the role, but emotional regulation might be one of the most important skills you'll ever develop as a CEO.

Your team doesn't just respond to your words. They respond to your state.

If you're anxious, they feel it.

If you're reactive, they become cautious.

If you're steady, they stabilize.

This doesn't mean pretending everything is fine. It means processing fear privately so you can lead responsibly in public.

One of the biggest mistakes leaders make is trying to power through stress without a system for releasing it. That stress doesn't disappear, it leaks. Into tone. Into decisions. Into culture.

And for me, into family.

In aviation, when conditions worsen, pilots slow down mentally. They rely on checklists. They reduce unnecessary variables. They don't speed up to outrun the wind.

Leadership demands the same discipline.

The Lift Is Already There

Here's the part that took me years to fully understand:

The resistance you're feeling isn't blocking your growth.

It's shaping it.

Adversity will visit the strong.

But it will live with the weak.

Strong leaders don't avoid pressure. They learn how to convert it into lift. They use resistance to clarify values, sharpen priorities, and simplify decisions.

Every hard season I've lived through as a CEO gave me something I didn't have before:

- Perspective
- Maturity
- Calm under fire
- A longer view of what actually matters

Those qualities don't come from easy stretches.

They come from headwinds.

What This Chapter Is Really Saying

If leadership feels heavy right now, that doesn't mean you're failing.

It means you're flying.

The goal isn't to eliminate the wind.

The goal is to stop being surprised by it.

Pressure is part of the job. Resistance is part of growth. And the leaders who last aren't the ones who never feel the strain, they're the ones who learn how to face it without losing themselves.

You don't take off by running with the wind.

You turn into it.

You trust your training.

And you let the resistance do what it was always meant to do.

Lift you.

Chapter 4

IMC - Flying in the Clouds

Pilots have a term for flying when you can't see anything outside the cockpit.

IMC - Instrument Meteorological Conditions.

It means you're in the clouds. No horizon. No ground reference. No visual confirmation that you're upright, or even pointed in the right direction. If you trust your instincts instead of your instruments, you can kill yourself in seconds.

Your body lies to you in IMC.

It tells you you're climbing when you're descending.

It tells you you're level when you're banking.

It tells you to correct something that doesn't need correcting.

The only way through is discipline.

You trust the instruments.

You ignore the noise.

You fly the airplane.

For me, COVID was IMC for leadership.

When the Horizon Disappeared

I remember exactly when it stopped feeling like a temporary disruption and started feeling like something else entirely.

At first, it was just news.

Then emails.

Then phone calls.

Then pressure, fast, loud, and contradictory.

The state was talking about shutdowns.

A county just north of us had already closed businesses.

Our county hadn't… yet.

From the outside, it probably looked like leadership. Decisions. Meetings. Calm updates. Reassurance.

From the inside, I was lost.

If we shut down for even a week or two, we wouldn't survive. We wouldn't make payroll. We wouldn't pay bills. We would go bankrupt. Years of work, gone.

But staying open meant something else entirely. It meant helping families pay bills. Keeping food on tables. Keeping healthcare. Keeping stability where we could.

We rearranged workstations overnight. Spaced people out. Sent anyone uncomfortable home. Asked anyone with symptoms to stay away. Created policies in real time while guidance changed daily.

Some employees wanted to come in. They knew their jobs and their families' stability depended on it. Others were terrified.

And then the emails started.

Messages telling me I was a murderer.

That I hated my employees.

That I only cared about money.

That there would be blood on my hands.

I would read those emails alone in my office. Then walk out and run a meeting. Then motivate a team. Then make another decision.

Was I making the wrong call?

I didn't know. I could only survive and keep moving forward.

I didn't have the luxury of collapsing.

Conflicting Instruments

In aviation, one of the most dangerous situations is when instruments disagree. When one says you're climbing and another says you're banking. If you chase all of them, you die.

Leadership during COVID felt exactly like that.

Public health guidance said one thing.

Financial reality said another.

Employee fear said something else entirely.

Media pressure amplified everything.

Every input demanded action. None came with certainty.

At night, I lay awake replaying decisions that hadn't even been made yet. Running scenarios. Imagining outcomes. Calculating damage.

Then morning would come.

And I'd get up.

Put on the same calm face.

Walk back into the clouds.

And tell everyone it was going to be okay.

The Lowest Point

Not long after COVID hit, we took another blow.

One of our top lead providers, representing between $90,000 and $150,000 a week in gross revenue, gave us one week's notice.

No more new students. No runway. Just gone.

Her own company was failing. She decided to go another direction.

At the same time, students from financed programs began defaulting. The finance company started coming back to us, demanding we buy back paper.

Revenue was dropping.

Liabilities were stacking.

Six figures of debt.

Fixed costs that couldn't be cut fast enough.

Payroll that didn't wait for explanations.

People told me to shut it down.

What they didn't see were the testimonials still coming in. Lives being changed. Students writing about breakthroughs. Employees showing up every day, trusting me to keep the plane in the air.

I had already put a lien on my home in a previous year to keep the company alive. Now the thought of losing everything, the company, our home, security for my wife and kids, was constant.

At home, bills were being missed. My wife was stressed. The kids needed things, lacrosse gear, dance classes, the normal life I wanted to give them.

And yet, from the outside?

Eight-figure business.

Awards.

The illusion of success.

That disconnect is where IMC becomes dangerous.

When the Body Lies

In IMC, pilots experience something called spatial disorientation. Your senses betray you. The plane feels wrong even when it's flying correctly. Panic sets in if you don't recognize what's happening.

That's what leadership felt like.

Every internal signal told me I was failing.

That I was the problem.

That removing myself would fix everything.

My thinking became narrow. Logical, but distorted.

I wasn't emotional.

I was resolved.

That's the part people don't understand about suicidal thinking. It doesn't always feel chaotic. Sometimes it feels calm. Final. Responsible. Clear.

Like you've found the answer.

The Discipline to Stay Alive

Pilots are trained for IMC long before they ever encounter it. Over and over, they're taught the same rule:

Trust the instruments, not your feelings.

Leadership needs the same discipline.

But here's the problem: most CEOs never build internal instruments. They rely on instinct, resilience, grit. And when instincts fail, there's nothing left to trust.

I didn't have the language for it then. I just knew something was breaking.

And like many leaders, I didn't say it out loud.

I couldn't.

So I kept flying.

What This Chapter Is Really Saying

IMC doesn't mean you're a bad pilot.

It means conditions changed.

Losing sight of the horizon doesn't mean you've lost your way.

It means you need different tools.

Leadership will put you in clouds you didn't plan for. You won't see the runway. You won't feel steady. And if you rely on how it feels, you'll make decisions that don't reflect reality.

The leaders who survive aren't the ones who never enter IMC.

They're the ones who learn to fly through it.

Even when they can't see where they're going yet.

Chapter 5

Payroll Before My Own Bills

There are moments in leadership that feel noble.

And then there are moments that feel quiet, heavy, and deeply personal. Moments no one applauds. Moments no one ever sees.

Payroll is one of them.

Most people think of payroll as a line item. A process. Something that just happens every two weeks because the system runs.

But when you're the CEO, payroll isn't abstract.

Payroll has names.

Payroll has families.

Payroll has mortgages, kids, tuition, groceries, and lives attached to it.

And when things get tight, payroll becomes a moral weight.

The Week the Math Didn't Work

There were weeks, more than I like to admit, when the numbers didn't line up cleanly.

Cash was coming in, but not fast enough. Revenue existed, but timing mattered. Expenses didn't care about timing. Neither did payroll.

I'd sit with spreadsheets open, running scenarios that all ended the same way:

If I paid myself, someone else didn't get paid.

If I protected my own bills, I risked hurting someone else.

So I made the choice many CEOs make silently.

I paid everyone else first.

Sometimes that meant skipping my own paycheck.

Sometimes it meant juggling bills at home.

Sometimes it meant pretending everything was fine when it wasn't.

My employees never knew.

That was the point.

The Hidden Agreement

There's an unspoken agreement leaders make with themselves:

I'll carry this so they don't have to.

At first, that feels right. Even honorable.

But over time, a line starts to blur. Because you're not just protecting people from fear, you're protecting them from reality. And you're isolating yourself in the process.

At home, the stress leaked out anyway.

Bills went unpaid.

Decisions got delayed.

The tension followed me through the door, even when I tried to leave it outside.

My wife felt it. She carried it with me. Quietly. Steadily. Without complaint, but not without cost.

That's one of the hardest truths of leadership:

Your family often pays for sacrifices they never agreed to make.

Looking Successful While Struggling

From the outside, the company looked successful.

Awards. Growth. Recognition. Eight figures.

From the inside, it felt like holding a structure together with discipline and duct tape. Constantly reinforcing load-bearing beams no one else noticed.

I'd stand in front of teams, motivating, reassuring, projecting confidence, while privately wondering how long we could keep doing this.

Company meetings were exhausting. Talking about wins. Celebrating progress. Holding the energy up.

All while knowing that within the hour I had a meeting with our property manager about a deficit, a bill, a lease payment they were demanding.

Who do I pay?

The lease?

A ten-thousand-dollar phone bill?

My employees?

Which decision buys us another week?

That gap between appearance and reality is dangerous.

It creates shame.

And shame is corrosive.

The Lie Leaders Tell Themselves

There's a lie many CEOs internalize when things get hard:

This is my fault.

Success gets shared.

Failure gets personalized.

For me, no one really knew. How could they? If they lost confidence, they'd leave, and without our employees, we wouldn't survive.

When revenue grows, it's the team.

When things break, it's you.

That belief doesn't just motivate, it isolates. It convinces you that asking for help is weakness. That admitting strain will erode confidence. That leadership means absorbing impact without reaction.

But leadership isn't about being unbreakable.

It's about being responsible.

And responsibility without boundaries eventually becomes self-destructive.

Calm Under Pressure

This is where a familiar principle came back to me again and again:

IN THE CHAOS, LOOK FOR THE CALMEST PERSON IN THE ROOM.

THAT'S YOUR LEADER.

Calm doesn't mean numb.

It doesn't mean detached.

It means regulated.

I learned to slow my reactions, even when the numbers scared me. To breathe. To think. To make decisions from principle instead of panic.

Not because I wasn't afraid.

But because fear couldn't be the one flying the plane.

What This Chapter Is Really Saying

If you've ever skipped your own paycheck to protect your team, you're not alone.

If you've ever carried financial stress quietly so others could feel secure, you're not weak.

But if you never put that weight down anywhere, if you never name it, share it, or process it, it will find a way out.

Leadership requires sacrifice.

It does not require self-destruction.

There is a difference.

And learning that difference may be one of the most important leadership skills you ever develop.

Chapter 6

Managing Personalities

No one tells you this when you become a CEO:

You don't really run a business.

You run people.

Strategies matter.

Numbers matter.

Systems matter.

But personalities decide whether any of it works.

A huge part of my job, probably the biggest part, has nothing to do with vision decks or financial models. It's listening. Translating. Absorbing. Calming. Redirecting.

It's emotional labor.

And it's constant.

The Emotional Thermostat

Every organization has a temperature.

Some days it's energized.

Some days it's anxious.

Some days it's quietly discouraged.

Whether you like it or not, you are the thermostat.

Your mood doesn't just stay in your head. It moves through the building, through Slack messages and emails, through meetings, through tone.

That's why I've come to believe this more than ever:

In the chaos, look for the calmest person in the room.

That's your leader.

Not the smartest.

Not the most charismatic.

The calmest.

Because psychology is more contagious than the flu.

If you bring anxiety into a room, it multiplies.

If you bring steadiness, it spreads.

Listening Without Fixing

One of the hardest lessons for me to learn was this:

Most people don't want solutions first.

They want to be understood.

As a CEO, your instinct is to fix. Solve. Optimize. Move forward. But when you do that too quickly, people don't feel led, they feel dismissed.

Managing personalities means learning how to listen without hijacking the conversation.

To let someone fully explain their frustration without immediately reframing it.

To sit in discomfort without rushing to resolution.

To hear emotion without taking it personally.

There's a reason that old YouTube video, "It's Not About the Nail" resonates so deeply. We've all been the person trying to fix something that first needed to be heard.

This took maturity. And patience. And restraint.

Because sometimes the most effective leadership move is not speaking at all.

Helping People See the Bigger Picture

(Without Losing Their Focus)

One of the great balancing acts of leadership is this:

Helping people understand the broader mission,

without distracting them from their role in it.

Not everyone needs the full picture.

Not everyone benefits from knowing everything.

Some people need context to stay motivated.

Others need clarity and boundaries to stay effective.

Part of managing personalities is knowing the difference.

Leadership isn't about giving everyone the same information.

It's about giving the right information to the right people at the right time.

That's not manipulation.

That's stewardship.

When Drama Wants the Controls

There's a quote that's followed me for years:

A man is only as big as the smallest thing that can take him out of the zone.

In leadership, that "smallest thing" is often emotional reactivity.

Drama wants the controls.

Ego wants the controls.

Fear wants the controls.

And if you let any of them fly the plane, you lose altitude fast.

I've learned that not every emotion deserves engagement.

Not every conflict needs escalation.

Not every complaint is a crisis.

Maturity in leadership is learning when to lean in, and when to stay centered and let the moment pass.

Culture Is Built in Micro-Moments

Culture isn't what you say in all-hands meetings.

It's how you respond when someone's upset.

How you handle conflict behind closed doors.

How you speak about people when they're not in the room.

Culture is built in moments when no one's watching.

That's why managing personalities matters so much. Every interaction is a signal. Every reaction teaches people what's safe, what's rewarded, and what's tolerated.

And here's the hard part:

You don't get days off from that responsibility.

The Invisible Fatigue

This kind of leadership is exhausting in a way that's hard to explain.

You carry other people's emotions.

You absorb their fears.

You regulate yourself so they don't have to.

And then you go home and do it again for your family.

This is where many leaders start to fray, not because they aren't capable, but because they don't have anywhere to set the weight down.

Work becomes love made visible.

But without boundaries, love can become depletion.

What This Chapter Is Really Saying

Managing personalities isn't a distraction from leadership.

It is leadership.

And it requires:

- Emotional discipline
- Perspective
- Patience
- And a deep understanding that your internal state shapes your external results

Or, as I've learned over time:

The outcome can only be as great as the energetic state in which you initiate the action.

If you want better outcomes, you don't start with strategy.

You start with state.

Chapter 7

Selling Rainbows and Unicorns

When we first started building Achieve Today more than a decade ago, most people didn't take what we did seriously.

Mindset.

Personal development.

High-performance habits.

To much of the business world, it sounded like fluff.

Woo-woo.

Rainbows and unicorns.

At the time, mindset coaching wasn't mainstream. It wasn't respected. It certainly wasn't considered a real business lever. Strategy was what mattered. Tactics. Funnels. Scripts. Playbooks.

Mindset was something people talked about when they didn't want to admit they didn't have a better answer.

Except we had seen something others hadn't.

The Pattern We Couldn't Ignore

Before Achieve Today, the first twelve years of my career were spent inside education, training, and coaching programs that focused almost entirely on strategy.

Same curriculum.

Same coaches.

Same material.

And yet, wildly different outcomes.

We could train two students side by side, give them identical tools, identical instruction, identical access, and one would succeed while the other would call the program a scam.

At first, like most organizations, we assumed it was the curriculum. So we tweaked it. Improved it. Rebuilt it.

But the pattern didn't change.

What changed outcomes wasn't information.

It was belief.

Resilience.

Commitment.

Follow-through.

Identity.

It wasn't that the strategies were broken.

It was that the person running them was.

That realization changed everything for me.

Why Strategy Isn't Enough

Here's the uncomfortable truth most leadership books avoid:

You don't rise to what you believe is possible.

You fall to what you believe you are worthy of.

I've watched this play out thousands of times. Working with more than 100,000 students around the world gave us the data to see it clearly.

People don't fail because they lack intelligence.

They fail because they quit early.

They fail because adversity convinces them the problem is external.

They fail because they don't trust themselves enough to persist.

As Og Mandino wrote:

"I will persist until I succeed.

I was not delivered unto this world in defeat...

I am a lion, and I refuse to talk, to walk, to sleep with the sheep."

That isn't motivation.

That's identity.

And identity determines behavior long before strategy ever does.

Betting on the Invisible

So we did something most people thought was backward.

We built a business that focused on mindset first.

We didn't lead with tactics.

We didn't promise shortcuts.

We worked on thought patterns, habits, resilience, and accountability.

And we paid the price for it early.

We were dismissed.

We were misunderstood.

We were told it wouldn't scale.

That people wouldn't pay for "intangibles."

But slowly, quietly, the results spoke.

Proof Before Permission

Our first clients weren't small names.

They were established authors and thought leaders. People like Joe Vitale, T. Harv Eker, Les Brown, and others, who already had massive audiences and proven programs.

They didn't come to us because their content was failing.

They came because we were able to offer one-one-one coaching at scale, and provide personal support to create new habits with their students.

When we stepped in and focused on mindset and accountability, something shifted.

Success rates improved.

Retention increased.

Student satisfaction climbed.

The pattern repeated again and again.

Eventually, other thought leaders reached out. Different industries. Same problem.

Great programs.

Inconsistent results.

Real estate brokerages.

E-commerce training.

Network marketing teams.

Entrepreneurship and business-building programs.

They all wanted to add mindset, high-performance habits, and one-on-one accountability, not as an add-on, but as a foundation.

The solution wasn't new strategy.

It was better psychology.

Expanding the Idea

As time went on, we saw opportunities to expand beyond personal development.

Real estate education.

Network marketing.

E-commerce.

Entrepreneurship.

Business building.

Different verticals. Same core issue.

People didn't fail because they didn't know what to do.

They failed because they didn't do it long enough, consistently enough, or with enough belief to push through resistance.

So we focused on accountability.

On high-performance mindset.

On removing limiting beliefs and reprogramming negative thought patterns.

We helped people build new habits.

That's when something I had heard before clicked for me:

Easy choices, hard life.

Hard choices, easy life.

Mindset work is the hard choice. It's uncomfortable. It forces responsibility. It removes excuses.

But it makes everything else easier.

Purple Cows and Perspective

When I was growing up, my family had a tradition.

Movie nights meant popcorn and purple cows, a simple shake made of grape juice and vanilla ice cream. Fun. Memorable. Ours.

Years later, I read The Milkshake Moment, the story of someone ordering a milkshake through room service and being told it wasn't available, until a high performer figured out how to make it happen anyway.

That story stuck with me.

High performers don't stop at no.

They figure it out.

Now, when I make purple cows with my own kids, it reminds me of both things at once, creativity and care. Performance and humanity.

That's what we were really building.

Not a business that sold information.

But one that helped people become the kind of person who could actually use it.

What This Chapter Is Really Saying

Selling rainbows and unicorns wasn't naïve.

It was early.

Mindset isn't soft.

It's foundational.

Every strategy runs through psychology.

Every system depends on belief.

Every outcome reflects identity.

Or as Tom Brady put it:

"To be successful at anything, you don't have to be special. You just have to be what most people aren't: consistent, determined, and willing to work for it."

Consistency.

Determination.

Willingness.

Those aren't tactics.

They're traits.

And traits are built long before results ever show up.

Chapter 8

Purple Cows

Some of the most important leadership lessons don't come from boardrooms.

They come from kitchens.

From couches.

From quiet moments that remind you who you were before the pressure showed up.

Growing up, my family had a tradition we called purple cows.

Grape juice and vanilla ice cream. That was it.

Movie nights weren't elaborate. No big production. Just us, a simple treat, and time together. It was ordinary, and unforgettable.

Finding a Way

Years later, I came across a story often referred to as the milkshake moment.

Someone orders a milkshake through room service and is told they don't have milkshakes. Most people would stop there.

But a high performer doesn't.

He asks if they have ice cream.

He asks if they have milk.

He asks them to bring both, along with an empty glass, so he can make his own.

It wasn't complicated.

It wasn't flashy.

It was intentional.

Room service realized what was happening after it was too late. They didn't solve the problem for the guest, they were stuck inside a box when they replied that milkshakes weren't on the menu.

How many people would go beyond the easy answer of "that's not possible" to deliver something memorable, not because it was convenient, but because it mattered?

That story always stuck with me.

Not because it was clever.

But because it revealed something deeper.

High Performers Figure It Out

Leadership, at its core, is the ability to say:

We'll find a way.

Not recklessly.

Not arrogantly.

But creatively. Responsibly. Humanly.

High performers don't get stuck on constraints. They don't need perfect conditions. They need commitment.

That mindset applies everywhere:

- To customers
- To employees
- To families
- To yourself

When people say, "That's not possible," great leaders ask, "*What is possible?*"

Why Small Things Matter More Than You Think

As Achieve Today grew, the business became more complex.

Bigger numbers.

Bigger decisions.

Bigger risks.

But the things that grounded me didn't get bigger.

They got smaller.

Moments with my kids.

Dinner with my wife.

Movie nights.

Purple cows.

Now, when I make them with my own kids, I'm reminded of something leadership culture rarely celebrates:

You don't lead well by becoming more impressive.

You lead well by staying connected.

Work is love made visible.

But love needs reminders.

Culture Is Built the Same Way

What's true at home is true in business.

Culture isn't built through grand gestures.

It's built through small, consistent signals.

The way you respond to a problem.

The way you treat someone when it would be easier not to care.

The extra effort that quietly says, You matter.

Those are the purple cows of leadership.

They don't show up on financial statements.

They don't win awards.

But they create loyalty, trust, and momentum that no strategy alone ever could.

Creativity Under Pressure

The milkshake story and the purple cow story share the same lesson:

Constraints don't kill creativity.

They force it.

Some of my best leadership decisions came when options were limited. When the answer wasn't obvious. When quitting would have been easier.

Those moments didn't require brilliance.

They required care.

Care for people.

Care for outcomes.

Care enough to try one more thing.

What This Chapter Is Really Saying

Leadership isn't just about surviving pressure.

It's about remembering why you're willing to.

In the middle of chaos, growth, responsibility, and stress, it's easy to lose sight of the small things that anchor you.

Purple cows matter.

They remind you:

- Who you are
- Who you're doing this for
- And that creativity and humanity still have a place in leadership

Even when the stakes are high.

Especially when they are.

Chapter 9

The Buyback Spiral

Most leadership crises don't arrive as explosions.

They arrive as math.

Quiet. Relentless. Unemotional math.

One problem rarely takes a company down.

It's what happens when problems start stacking, each one amplifying the next.

That's the spiral.

When One "Yes" Becomes a Hundred "Owes"

Financed programs look great on paper.

You sell a program.

A finance company purchases the paper.

You get cash now.

The student pays over time.

It works, until it doesn't.

When students began defaulting, the finance company didn't call the students first.

They called us.

Suddenly, revenue that had already been counted, planned for, and spent wasn't revenue anymore. It was liability. Paper we had to buy back. Money that had to be returned.

At the same time, new sales were slowing.

Then dropping.

Then falling off a cliff.

The numbers stopped behaving.

And when numbers stop behaving, leadership becomes deeply personal.

The Compounding Effect

Here's what people don't understand about cash flow stress:

It's not just about money.

It's about timing.

And timing doesn't negotiate.

Payroll doesn't wait for collections.

Vendors don't care about explanations.

Debt doesn't pause while you regroup.

Sales slowed week after week. Revenue dropped. Buybacks increased as defaults rose. The post-COVID economy tightened, and we were caught in it.

Each buyback made the next one harder.

Each slow week tightened the following one.

And fixed costs, the ones you can't unwind quickly, just sat there, unmoved.

We couldn't even lay off enough people to keep up, nor would we want to. At this point laying someone off was cutting bone. We had already gotten as lean as possible.

That's when stress stops being situational and starts becoming ambient.

It's everywhere.

In every decision.

In every conversation.

It follows you home.

The Stories You Start Telling Yourself

When things spiral, the most dangerous thing isn't the numbers.

It's the story you attach to them.

I started believing:

- *I missed something obvious.*
- *A better CEO wouldn't be here.*
- *Everyone else could fix this faster than I can.*

That's when this truth shows up, uninvited:

You will succeed or fail based on the stories you tell yourself and others.

And in isolation, those stories turn dark… fast.

When Leadership Becomes a Mask

The pressure didn't make me stop leading.

It made me lead harder.

More positivity.

More resolve.

More "we've got this."

I was determined not to let the stress leak into the organization. People depended on me. Believed in me.

So I doubled down on strength.

But strength without release turns into rigidity.

I wasn't lying to anyone.

But I wasn't telling the whole truth either.

And that's a lonely place to live.

The Illusion of Control

Here's something leaders don't like to admit:

There are moments when you're no longer steering.

You're correcting, constantly, just to stay upright.

I kept telling myself:

If I can just get through this week...

If I can just solve this next issue...

But the weeks didn't get easier.

The problems didn't resolve cleanly.

They multiplied.

And the spiral tightened.

Perspective Comes Later

Years later, with distance and experience, I can see this season more clearly.

At the time, it felt like failure.

Now, it looks like refinement.

As Orison Swett Marden wrote:

"Success is not measured by what you accomplish, but by the opposition you have encountered, and the courage with which you have maintained that struggle against overwhelming odds."

I didn't know it then, but I was being shaped.

Not into a better strategist.

Into a steadier leader.

Chapter 10

The Waterfall

The darkest moments don't always feel dark.

Sometimes they feel calm.

Resolved.

Logical.

That's what surprised me the most.

This wasn't panic.

It wasn't chaos.

It wasn't an emotional breakdown.

It felt like clarity.

When the Math Turns Inward

By that point, the pressure had been constant for so long it stopped feeling temporary.

Revenue had dropped.

Buybacks had stacked.

Fixed costs refused to move.

Payroll still arrived on schedule, the lease still needed paid, an unrelenting reminder that time doesn't care how heavy things feel.

At home, the stress showed up quietly.

Missed bills.

Delayed decisions.

Conversations that ended in silence instead of solutions.

My wife was strong, stronger than anyone should have to be, but I could feel the strain I was putting on her. On our family.

At work, I kept doing what leaders do.

I showed up.

I motivated.

I reassured.

I made decisions.

From the outside, nothing looked broken.

Inside, everything felt like it was my fault.

That's the lie leadership whispers when things go wrong:

Success belongs to everyone.

Failure belongs to you.

And if failure belongs to you, then the solution must, too.

The Logic Trap

I didn't spiral emotionally.

I reasoned.

I told myself:

- If I'm the problem, removing the problem helps everyone.

- If I'm not here, payroll gets easier.

- If I'm gone, the company can find a leader who can solve this.

- If I'm gone, insurance money helps my family, and they don't lose our home.

- If I'm gone, they don't have to feel my stress.

- If I'm gone, the pressure stops. Finally. Peace. I need to feel peace.

It felt responsible.

It felt unselfish.

It felt… finished.

That's what makes this kind of thinking so dangerous.

It doesn't feel like despair.

It feels like duty.

The Morning You Don't Forget

That morning, I hugged my kids longer than usual before they left for school.

Not dramatically.

Not obviously.

Just long enough to remember the feeling.

I hugged my wife and told her I loved her. Then I left for work.

In my mind, I was running a final checklist.

Things to finish.

Things to close.

Things to hand off.

I knew where I was going.

A canyon just minutes from the office.

A waterfall I had always loved.

A place that felt quiet. Removed. Away from the noise I felt responsible for.

I went into the office and tried to work.

Tried to act normal.

I waited for a moment when I could slip away.

The emotion was almost unbearable, not frantic, just heavy. Settled.

I had thought through every step up the trail.

Every moment on the climb.

Every feeling I expected to feel.

I was ready.

The Interruption

As I walked to my car to begin the short drive up the canyon, my phone rang.

It was my business partner and best friend, Aaron.

He lived in Idaho. We only saw each other every few months. He wasn't in the daily pressure, the conversations, the faces. He had no idea where my thoughts had gone.

He asked one simple question:

"How are you doing?"

I said what leaders say.

"Fine."

He paused.

"Usually when someone says they're fine," he said, "it means the opposite."

Something cracked.

Not dramatically.

Not all at once.

Just enough.

I told him about the pressure.

The fear.

The uncertainty.

The numbers.

The emails.

The exhaustion.

The feeling that I was failing everyone.

He listened.

Then he said something I still carry with me:

"Josh, you've led this company through its most profitable and successful years. You are a great leader. And I know you'll get us through this."

No fixing.

No minimizing.

No advice.

Just truth.

One More Thing to Do

After that call, I remembered a meeting I had scheduled, a software demo with a potential client.

Something about missing that meeting felt wrong.

Not dramatic.

Just… unfinished.

So instead of starting my car, I turned around.

I walked back into the office.

I got on the Zoom call.

It was hard.

I went to work.

That call saved my life.

Aaron didn't know what he interrupted, not then. Not for years. And even now, I don't think he fully realizes how close that moment was.

But that's often how this works.

It isn't a grand rescue.

It's a small interruption.

A voice.

A question.

A reason to stay one more hour.

What This Chapter Is Really Saying

If you're a leader who's ever thought,

They'd be better off without me.

That thought is not clarity.

It's distortion.

It's pressure turning inward.

It's responsibility without perspective.

It's isolation convincing you that removal is the solution.

It isn't.

Leadership can feel unbearable when you carry it alone.

But unbearable does not mean unfixable.

Sometimes survival looks like courage.
Sometimes it looks like postponing a decision.
Like taking one more meeting.
Like answering one phone call honestly.

And sometimes it looks like choosing to stay, long enough for the clouds to thin. There's something I've felt at times since that day, a strange frustration that I failed at what I planned.

Leaders hate to fail.

Even at things like that.

But if I had to fail at something, I'm grateful it was that.

Because things got better.

Chapter 11

The Call That Saved Me

I used to think what saved me was timing.

Right place.

Right moment.

Right phone call.

But over time, I've come to understand something deeper.

What saved me wasn't luck.

It was connection.

The Power of Interruption

Leadership has a dangerous side effect:

Isolation disguised as strength.

The higher you go, the fewer people interrupt your thinking. Not because they don't care, but because they assume you're fine. Capable. In control.

That's why interruption matters so much.

The call from Aaron didn't magically solve our problems. It didn't change the numbers. It didn't erase the pressure.

What it did was interrupt a story that had narrowed too far.

That's the real danger zone for leaders, not stress, not fear, not even failure.

It's narrow thinking.

When the world shrinks to a single conclusion.

When options disappear.

When responsibility turns into self-erasure.

That's when interruption saves lives.

The Question That Matters

Aaron didn't ask about revenue.

He didn't ask about strategy.

He didn't ask about the company.

He asked about me.

"How are you doing?"

And when I gave the automatic answer, he didn't accept it.

That's leadership too.

Knowing when not to move on.

Knowing when to stay with the question.

Most people don't need advice in their darkest moments.

They need presence.

Safe People Aren't Accidental

One of the biggest lessons I took from that day is this:

You don't build safe people in a crisis.

You build them before one.

Safe people are the ones who:

- Can hear the truth without panicking
- Don't need you to perform
- Aren't invested in your image
- Care more about you than the role you carry

For me, that has always started with my wife, Raelene.

She's been my constant. My grounding force. The person who sees past titles, past pressure, past performance. She didn't fall in love with a CEO.

She fell in love with a human.

And that matters more than most leaders realize.

My partnership with Aaron mattered too, not just professionally, but personally. He believed in me when I couldn't access belief for myself. For over 25 years we worked together and he always believed in my ability before anyone else.

That belief didn't inflate me.

It stabilized me.

Building the Two-Person Rule

In aviation, there are tasks you never perform without a checklist. Not because pilots are weak, but because humans under pressure are fallible.

Leadership deserves the same respect.

Every CEO needs a two-person rule:

- At least one person who has permission to challenge your internal narrative
- Someone who can say, That's not true, when your thinking turns against you
- Someone who will ask the real question, and stay long enough to hear the real answer

This isn't about dependency.

It's about design.

Strong systems don't rely on heroics.

They rely on redundancy.

Courage Looks Quiet

We talk a lot about courage in leadership.

Standing firm.

Making hard calls.

Taking responsibility.

But one of the bravest things a leader can do is this:

Tell the truth to the right person at the right time.

Not publicly.

Not dramatically.

Quietly. Honestly.

That day, courage wasn't me pushing through.

It was me answering the phone.

It was me staying.

Gratitude Changes the Equation

There's a quote I've always loved by Michael J. Fox:

With gratitude, optimism is sustainable.

Looking back now, I don't feel embarrassment about that day.

I feel gratitude.

Gratitude that the call came when it did.

Gratitude that someone cared enough to ask twice.

Gratitude that I had one more reason to stay.

Gratitude doesn't erase hardship.

But it reframes it.

What This Chapter Is Really Saying

If you're a leader reading this and thinking, I don't have anyone like that, then this chapter is your signal.

Build it.

Not tomorrow.

Not when things get worse.

Now.

Decide who gets access to the real you.

Give them permission to interrupt you.

Make it safe for someone to ask the question you might not want to answer.

Because leadership isn't about being untouchable.

It's about being reachable.

Chapter 12

Values in a Crisis

You don't really know your values when things are going well.

When revenue is up, teams are happy, and decisions have upside, values are easy to claim. They sound good on walls and websites. They make for great onboarding decks.

The real test comes when there are no good options left.

That's when values stop being words and start becoming weights.

When Every Option Costs Something

During our hardest seasons, there were days when every decision hurt someone.

If we cut costs, people lost jobs.

If we didn't, the company bled.

If we stayed open, people were afraid.

If we closed, people couldn't pay their bills.

There were no clean answers.

Just tradeoffs.

That's what leadership really is in a crisis, not choosing between good and bad, but between bad and worse, while still being able to look at yourself in the mirror.

I learned quickly that strategy won't save you in those moments.

Values will.

Values Aren't What You Say

They're What You're Willing to Pay For

Here's something I didn't understand early enough:

Values are expensive.

If they don't cost you something, they aren't values. They're preferences.

Compassion costs time and emotional energy.

Integrity costs convenience.

Honesty costs comfort.

Optimism costs effort.

And in a crisis, values often cost money.

There were moments when it would have been easier to say less. To soften the truth. To delay hard conversations. To make things look better than they were.

But every time I did that, even slightly, the cost showed up later, with interest.

So I learned to come back to a simple question:

What decision can I live with, even if it doesn't work out?

That question doesn't guarantee success.

But it preserves integrity.

Calm as a Moral Obligation

Earlier in this book, I shared this idea:

In the chaos, look for the calmest person in the room. That's your leader.

Over time, I realized something else:

Calm isn't just a leadership skill.

It's a moral obligation.

When people are scared, they don't need certainty, they need steadiness. They need someone who can hold tension without transmitting it. Someone who can absorb fear without amplifying it.

Calm doesn't mean pretending. It means regulating yourself so others can function.

That's values in motion.

When Values Become the Compass

There's a thought that's followed me for years:

Almost every successful person begins with two beliefs:

The future can be better than the present, and I have the power to make it so.

In a crisis, those beliefs are tested relentlessly.

Values are what keep you oriented when the future isn't visible and the present feels unbearable. They give you direction even when you don't have a map.

For me, values became the compass when the instruments were noisy.

When I didn't know what the outcome would be, I could still choose how we got there.

Integrity Over Image

One of the hardest leadership lessons I learned was this:

You can protect your image, or you can protect your values.

You usually can't do both.

There were times when being honest made me look weaker than I wanted. When choosing people over profit invited criticism. When staying aligned with our mission cost us speed.

But every time I chose values over image, something subtle happened.

Trust deepened.

Culture stabilized.

And internally, I could breathe again.

In time, that alignment showed up in ways I couldn't have predicted. We were ranked a Top Workplace in our state every year for over a decade. We were recognized by the United States Senate for our company culture and contribution to our state. Not long after the heaviest times I was recognized as the Top CEO in Utah by the Salt Lake Tribune.

What few people knew was what it cost to get there.

Leadership isn't about being admired.

It's about being aligned.

The Energy You Initiate With Matters

There's another truth I've come to live by:

The outcome can only be as great as the energetic state in which you initiate the action.

When decisions come from fear, they create more fear.

When they come from ego, they create resistance.

When they come from values, they create stability, even when they're painful.

That doesn't mean outcomes are always good.

It means they're clean.

What This Chapter Is Really Saying

If you're leading through a crisis right now, this matters:

You don't need perfect answers.

You need anchored decisions.

Values are not there to make leadership easy.

They're there to make it endurable.

When everything else is stripped away, certainty, praise, momentum, values are what remain.

And if you let them guide you, they will do something powerful:

They will give you back your sense of self.

Chapter 13

Turning Skyward

I wish I could tell you that leadership gets easier.

It doesn't.

But it does get clearer.

After everything, after the pressure, the clouds, the spiral, the interruption, I didn't come back as a different person. I came back as a more honest one.

More grounded.

More aware.

More deliberate.

Leadership didn't stop being heavy.

It stopped being confusing.

What Surviving Taught Me

Survival has a way of stripping things down to what actually matters.

Not titles.

Not accolades.

Not appearances.

What matters is:

- Who you are when no one is watching
- How you talk to yourself when things go wrong
- Whether your leadership is sustainable, for you, not just the company

I learned that strength isn't about being fearless.

Fear is part of the job.

The real work is deciding what you do with it.

Fear Isn't the Enemy

There's a passage I've always loved because it finally put words to something I felt but couldn't explain:

That's the thing about fear.

It can be powerful. It can rule a life, steal freedom, and cause pain. Or it can be vanquished, one glorious decision after another… Even the best are really only fearless one triumph at a time.

Fear doesn't disappear when you succeed.

It just changes shape.

And courage isn't the absence of fear, it's the willingness to keep choosing forward motion anyway.

Leadership will always put you at the edge of something uncertain. That edge doesn't mean you're failing.

It means you're alive in the work.

The goal was never to eliminate fear.

The goal was to make it irrelevant.

Leadership After the Storm

After everything I've lived through, here's what I know now:

Leadership is not about never breaking.

It's about knowing how to repair.

It's not about always being certain.

It's about staying aligned when certainty disappears.

And it's not about being admired.

As Lao Tzu said:

"A leader is best when people barely know he exists, when his work is done, his aim fulfilled, they will say: We did it ourselves."

There's a quote that's followed me most of my life:

"When once you have tasted flight you will forever walk the earth with your eyes turned skyward, for there you have been, and there you will always long to return." —Leonardo da Vinci

I didn't understand it fully when I first heard it.

I do now.

Because once you've flown through real pressure, once you've been in the clouds, felt the wind push sideways, questioned your own capacity, and still landed, you're never quite the same.

Leadership does that to you.

What Surviving Changes

I'm still a CEO.

I still carry responsibility.

I still face uncertainty.

But I don't carry it the same way.

I no longer believe leadership is about being unbreakable.

I no longer believe calm means feeling nothing.

I no longer confuse pressure with failure.

What changed wasn't the environment.

It was my relationship to it.

What I Know Now

If I could sit across from every CEO reading this book and say a few things plainly, it would be these:

- **You are not behind.**
  Leadership is a long game. What feels late is often just on time.
- **You are not broken.**
  Feeling the weight means you're carrying something that matters.
- **You don't rise to what you believe is possible.**
  You fall to what you believe you are worthy of.
- And you are worthy of support, clarity, and a future that doesn't cost you your soul.
- **Consistency beats intensity.**
  As Tom Brady said, success doesn't require being special, just consistent, determined, and willing to work for it.

- **Finishing matters.**
  Stopping at third adds no more to the score than striking out.
- **You will succeed or fail based on the stories you tell yourself.**
  Choose them carefully. They build the runway under your feet.

As Bo Eason put it:

"You will succeed or fail based on the stories you tell yourself and others."

The Leader You're Becoming

There's a quiet confidence that comes from having been through something you didn't think you'd survive, and discovering that you did.

Not because you were fearless.

But because you stayed.

Stayed in the work.

Stayed in the conversation.

Stayed alive to possibility.

That kind of leadership doesn't show up on résumés.

But it shows up everywhere else.

In your presence.

In your decisions.

In your ability to stay calm when others can't.

After the Storm

The company didn't collapse.

We kept going.

We rebuilt.

We adapted.

Today, Achieve Today is still here. Still growing. Still changing lives. Thousands of coaching sessions every week. Testimonials still arriving, real people, real breakthroughs, real impact.

From the outside, it looks like success.

From the inside, it looks like perspective.

Because I no longer confuse pressure with failure.

I no longer confuse exhaustion with weakness.

And I no longer confuse leadership with silence.

The Long View

There's a quote I've always loved:

"What the caterpillar calls the end of the world, the master calls a butterfly."

When you're in the middle of the storm, it never feels transformational. It feels like loss. Confusion. Failure.

Only later does perspective arrive.

And when it does, you realize something quietly profound:

Adversity didn't come to destroy you.

It came to shape you.

As another truth reminds us:

Adversity will visit the strong. But it will live with the weak.

Strong doesn't mean unbreakable.

It means willing.

What Success Really Requires

Leadership isn't about brilliance.

It's about persistence.

Og Mandino captured it perfectly:

"I will persist until I succeed."

Not because it's easy.

Not because it's guaranteed.

But because quitting isn't who you are.

Turning Skyward

There's a reason this book keeps coming back to flight.

Because flying teaches you something leadership eventually demands:

You don't eliminate headwinds.

You don't control weather.

You don't always see the runway.

You fly anyway.

And when conditions get rough, you don't turn away from the wind.

You turn into it.

Once you've carried real responsibility, real people, real consequences, you don't go back to shallow living.

You see differently.

You choose differently.

You lead differently.

Final Takeaways — Your Flight Plan

If you take nothing else from this book, take this with you:

- Build your **two-person rule**. Decide now who gets access to the real you.
- Regulate your state before you make decisions. Energy initiates outcomes.
- Anchor to **values**, not optics. Image fades. Integrity lasts.
- Name pressure early. Silence doesn't make you strong, it makes you alone.
- **Stay.** Even when leaving feels logical.

And keep this in mind:

"Remember that guy who gave up? Neither does anybody else."

Your life matters more than your company.

Your family matters more than your title.

And your leadership is strongest when it's human.

One Last Thought

You didn't step into leadership because it was easy.

You stepped into it because you believed something mattered enough to carry.

So when the wind picks up again, and it will, remember this:

You were never meant to outrun it.

You were meant to face it.

And let it lift you.

Epilogue

A Letter to the Leader

If you're reading this, it means you stayed.

You kept going long enough to finish a book that didn't promise shortcuts or hacks, only truth. That alone tells me something about you.

You're not afraid of responsibility.

You're not running from pressure.

And you care deeply about doing this right.

Leadership will never stop testing you. There will be new headwinds, new seasons of uncertainty, new moments where the picture looks wrong and the runway disappears. That's not a flaw in the path, it is the path.

I want you to remember something when those moments come:

You were never meant to carry this alone.

You don't need to be the strongest person in every room.

You don't need to have every answer.

You don't need to earn rest by suffering first.

You are allowed to be human and lead well.

If you ever find yourself thinking that removing yourself would solve everything, pause. That thought is not wisdom, it's pressure lying to you. Your presence matters more than your perfection.

Stay long enough for the clouds to thin.

Answer the phone.

Tell the truth to someone safe.

Take one more step.

Leadership is not about being fearless.

It's about choosing to fly anyway.

—*Josh*

About the Author

Josh Christopherson is the CEO of Achieve Today, one of the largest coaching fulfillment companies in the industry, delivering more than 1,400 one-on-one coaching sessions each week for leading brands across business, real estate, and personal development. Over the past 25 years, he has built and led multiple companies in education and technology, helping serve more than 150,000 students in over 70 countries.

Josh has spent his career working at the intersection of performance, psychology, and leadership, supporting organizations as they scale. Under his leadership, Achieve Today has been recognized nationally for both innovation and culture, earning repeated "Best Places to Work" honors and recognition for leadership and impact.

This book was written not as a business manual, but as an honest account of the invisible pressures leaders carry, and the lessons learned while carrying them.

Outside of work, Josh is a husband, father of three, and lifelong pilot. His love of aviation continues to shape how he thinks about leadership, pressure, and what it means to stay steady when conditions aren't ideal.

Acknowledgements

This book exists because of people who showed up in quiet ways at the right moments. To Adam Mortimer, Director of Coaching and Training at Achieve Today, thank you for unknowingly giving me the courage to finally tell this story. You didn't know what you were unlocking, but your belief in coaching pushed me to sit down and finish something I'd been carrying for years. To the clients and partners who trusted us long before this work was understood, especially Joe Vitale, whose body of work has shaped generations, and Dustin Worthen, a friend and steady leader whose example continues to remind me what aligned leadership looks like, thank you. To Aaron Peterson, my business partner and friend, thank you for the steady belief, perspective, and presence that often mattered more than solutions, and for showing me what resilient leadership looks like in practice. To my partners Rod and Andy for your unwavering support over the difficult years. And most importantly, to my wife and children: you carried more than you should have had to, believed when I struggled to, and loved me through every version of this journey. This book may carry my name, but it is built on your strength.

Leadership Checklist

The Invisible Game: A Flight Plan for CEOs

Use this when pressure is high. Print it. Keep it close.

1) BEFORE YOU DECIDE

☐ Have I regulated my emotional state first?

☐ Am I reacting to fear or responding from values?

☐ What story am I telling myself right now, and is it true?

"The outcome can only be as great as the energetic state in which you initiate the action."

2) WHEN THE WIND PICKS UP

☐ Am I trying to run with the wind, or turn into it?

☐ What is this resistance asking me to adjust?

☐ What can I control today?

Headwinds create lift, if you face them.

3) IN THE CLOUDS (IMC)

☐ What are my "instruments" right now? (values, data, counsel)

☐ Which signals should I ignore?

☐ Who do I trust when visibility is gone?

Trust instruments, not feelings.

4) WHEN IT FEELS PERSONAL

☐ Am I confusing responsibility with blame?

☐ Would I judge another CEO as harshly as I'm judging myself?

☐ What would calm leadership look like in this moment?

In the chaos, look for the calmest person in the room.

5) PEOPLE & CULTURE

☐ Am I listening to understand, or to fix?

☐ Who needs context vs. clarity right now?

☐ What am I modeling with my tone?

Psychology is contagious.

6) YOUR TWO-PERSON RULE

☐ Who has permission to ask how I'm really doing?

☐ Who can interrupt my worst thinking?

☐ Have I actually told them they have this permission?

Strong systems rely on redundancy, not heroics.

7) WHEN THINGS GET DARK

☐ Have I delayed irreversible decisions?

☐ Have I reached out to someone safe?

☐ What is one small reason to stay today?

Narrow thinking is a warning sign, not a conclusion.

8) THE LONG GAME

☐ Am I acting from integrity over image?

☐ Will I respect this decision later, even if it doesn't work?

☐ What does persistence look like today?

"I will persist until I succeed."